PREFACE

The purpose of this text is to provide the intermediate drummer with a collection of musical studies which will 1. increase his technical ability and 2. develop musicianship.

Musical Studies for the Intermediate Snare Drummer is divided into two sections. Both sections are saturated with dynamic markings in order to cultivate the student's sense of musical expressiveness. The first section contains fifteen studies in both simple and compound time. No rolls or embellishments are used in this section in order to allow the student time to become completely familiar with dynamics and accents. The second section contains an equal number of studies but makes extensive use of flams, drags and rolls of varying duration.

It is my sincere hope that this book will provide the serious student with an effective and musical approach to drumming.

© Copyright 1971 by JOEL ROTHMAN,
International Copyright Secured

DEDICATED TO MY PARENTS

Most of the dynamic changes in this study happen suddenly and without warning *(subito)*. Be sure to look ahead and be ready for quick dynamic changes.

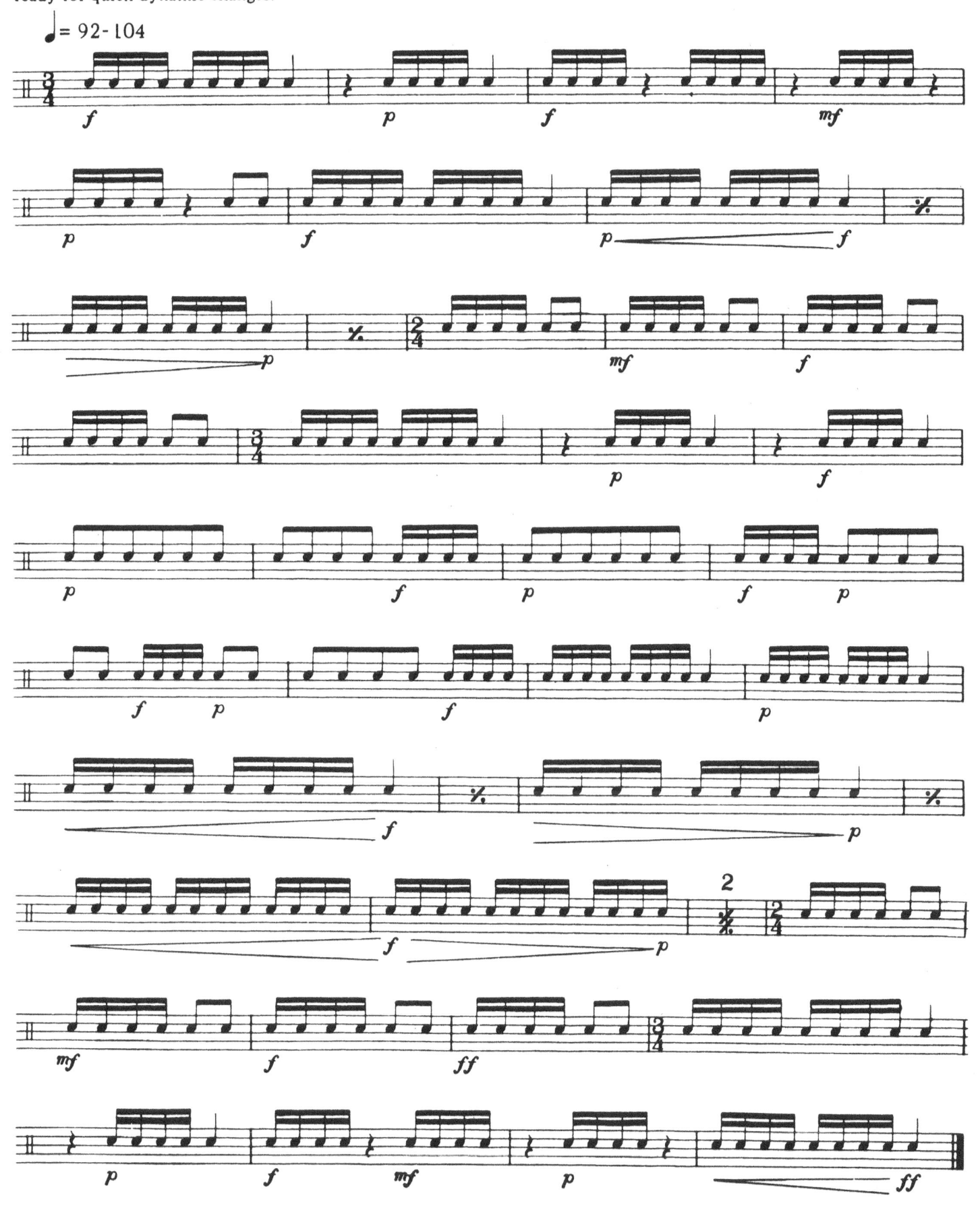

Note the difference between the two types of accents used in this study. Accents must be played in relation to the dynamic level in which they occur.

Again, sudden dynamic changes are common in this exercise. Make sure that the *cresc. poco a poco* is gradual and even; do not reach **ff** prematurely.

This study combines elements from the previous pages. Observe carefully, dynamics and accents.

The time signature of 5/4 is not uncommon in music of today; count accurately. The *crescendo* from beginning to end must be gradual and even.

♩ = 116-126

ppp cresc.poco a poco al Fine

fff

One of the most frequently misplayed rhythms in our musical vocabulary is that of the dotted eighth-sixteenth. To insure rhythmic accuracy, sub-dividing (in this case counting 1 e & a) should be used.

Be sure that the beat does not change when changing the rhythm from duplets to triplets etc. This study will require concentrated practice to produce rhythmic precision.

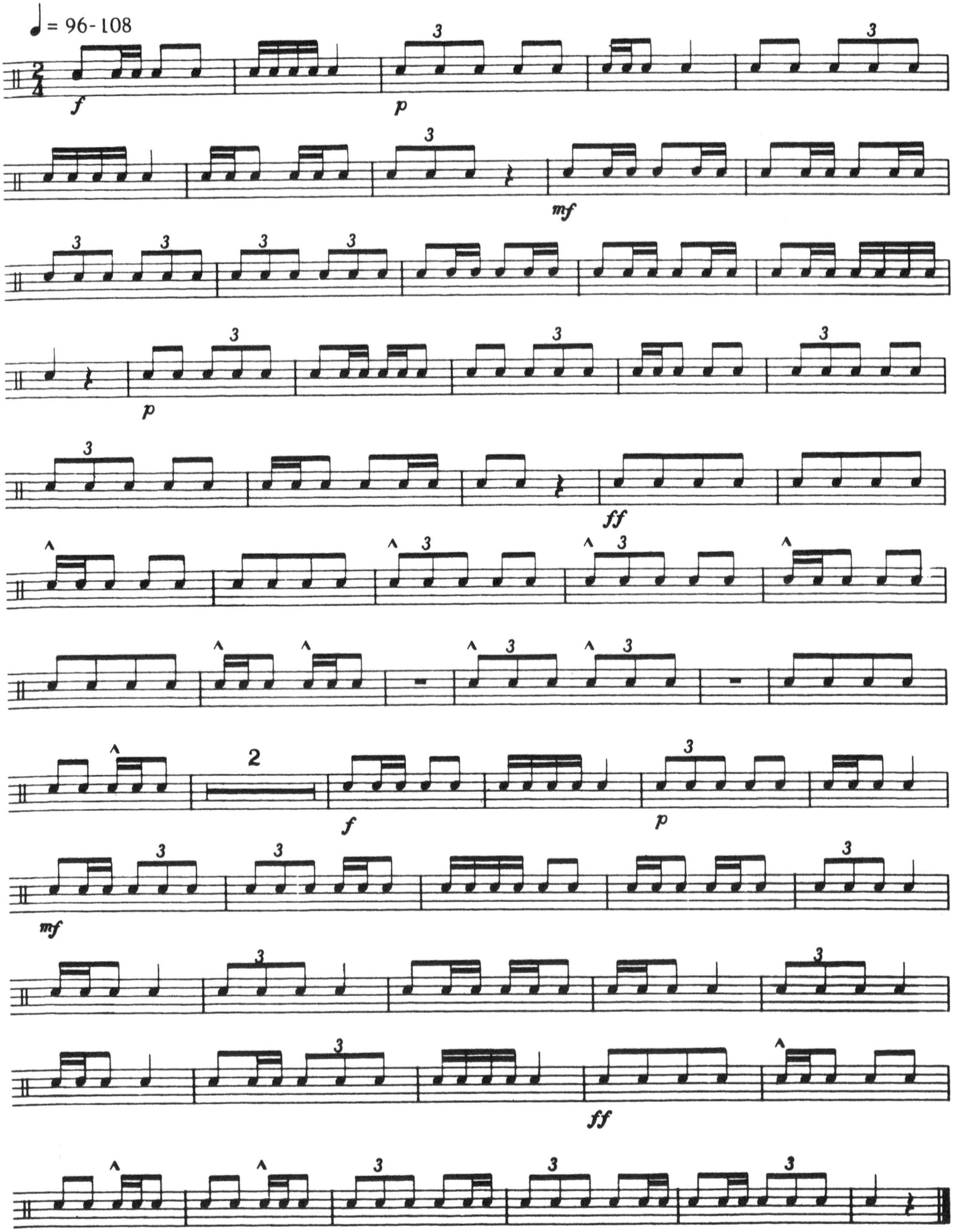

The interplay between sixteenth and eighth notes and triplets in this study is rather tricky. Sub-divide carefully.

♩ = 100-112

12

The sixteenth note triplets in this study must be played dynamically even and rhythmically precise.

♩ = 88-100

mf sempre

This is the first of several exercises which uses the eighth note as the metric denominator. These exercises should completely familiarize the student with rhythms characteristic of 3/8 – 6/8 – 9/8 and 12/8. Note the difference in this study between ♪♩.♩, ♩.♪♩ and ♩♩.♪

14

This study begins in a characteristic march tempo in two, which gradually *ritards* to a slow section to be played in six. Both the *ritard* and the *accelerando* should be gradual and even until the desired tempo is reached.

The measures of rest in this exercise come at awkward places. Make sure that the rhythms preceding these empty measures do not "spill over."

♩. = 60-72

Try to make the swells (< >) in this study as smooth as possible. A smooth contour of sound should be achieved.

♩. = 72-84

A combination of elements from the preceding studies are found in this exercise. The pulse remains steady throughout the many meter changes. Changes in meter are quite common in today's music.

18

This study deals primarily with rolls of varying duration. In concert band or orchestral drumming, rolls are not measured. The desired effect is a smooth, continuous sound.

♩ = 92-108

This is the first use of flams in this book. Flams should have a sharp, clean sound, not too open and not in unison (both sticks striking together). I have left the sticking up to the student and teacher. However, the end result must be a perfectly executed flam.

Drags or ruffs are quite characteristic of many drum parts. They may be played "open" so that all notes are distinguishable (common in rudimental drumming) or "closed" so as to make a short, sharp roll sound. In this study the ruffs should be played closed.

Again in this study the ruffs should be played "closed." Note the marking *sfz*. It means with a sudden, strong accent.

Once again, this exercise utilizes changing meters. The pulse is constant, only the number of beats in the measure changes. Be sure to make all sixteenth note rhythms as even as possible.

By playing on different areas of the drum a variety of sounds may be produced. The edge of the drum is often used to execute extremely soft passages. The center of the drum produces a dry sound. Playing on the rim is an effect often called for in marches and show music.

24

Note the difference between ♪. ♫ and ♫ ♪.. Be sure to sub divide for rhythmic precision.

As previously stated, great care should be taken in changing from duplets to triplets, etc. Be careful not to accent the end of a roll unless an accent is indicated (especially ♩♪).

When the end of a roll is also the beginning of a rhythmic figure ($\xi \quad \sqrt{}\sqrt{}\sqrt{}\sqrt{}$) it is often quite difficult not to accent that figure. Great care must be taken to avoid this practice.

This study contains many elements previously discussed. Rhythmic precision and good sound should be the goal of this page.

28

In playing the figure ♪♪♪, the student must be completely relaxed. This is a difficult figure and must be played correctly. Tightening up will only cause the triplet to be played incorrectly. All of the triplet figures must be perfectly even.

This exercise should be played "in 1." Start slowly in order to learn the dynamics and rhythms and gradually increase the tempo until a relaxed feeling of "1" is reached.

♩. = 66-76

f sempre

This is a rather characteristic 6/8 study. Since the dynamic level is constant, the accents must also be constant. This is an important point. The student must consciously establish a dynamic level for accents.

♩. = 72-80

mf

A great deal of control is necessary in order to achieve a "clean" sound during the soft passages of this study. Playing near the edge of the drum will help to produce this sound.

32

The main theme of this study, measure 1, is brought back several times. Be sure it is played the same on each restatement. Again, as in the last exercise, the extremely soft passages may be played on the edge.